My NAKED SOUL

SPILLING My GUTS

Crystal Joy Browne Webb

WESTBOW
PRESS®
A DIVISION OF THOMAS NELSON
& ZONDERVAN

WestBow Press books may be ordered through booksellers or by contacting:

WestBow Press
A Division of Thomas Nelson & Zondervan
1663 Liberty Drive
Bloomington, IN 47403
www.westbowpress.com
844-714-3454

ISBN: 978-1-9736-9895-1 (sc)
ISBN: 978-1-9736-9894-4 (e)

Library of Congress Control Number: 2023909576

Print information available on the last page.

WestBow Press rev. date: 5/31/2023

Thanks to:

Mother and father, Rhonda and Dave

Husband Danny

Sister Donna

Good friends Mike and Deb

As you read these words, look to Jesus…

You know the beautiful sunrays when they filter through the clouds and shine down to the earth in the distance? You can still see the clouds, but the beauty is in the sunlight. The gorgeous rays wouldn't exist if there were no clouds. Yes, my friend, undergo the clouds. But focus on the sunrays…

And praise the God who made them.

Psalm 8:3-4
"When I look at Your heavens, the work of Your fingers, the moon and the stars, which You have set in place, what is man that you are mindful of him, and the son of man that you care for him?"

Contents

Sizzlin'
Sampler

The Appetizer

This diverse Sizzlin' Sampler is an opportunity
to whet your appetite for all chapter themes!

Chapter 1
Sizzlin' Sampler: The Appetizer

"Stuff 'n' Things"

Psalm 116:1-2 NIV

I love the Lord,
for he heard my voice;
He heard my **cry for mercy.**
Because <u>He turned his ear to me,</u>
I will call on him as long as I live.

Check This Out

Just picture this. You're standing at a public bathroom sink, minding
your own business. You hear a toilet flush from a stall behind you.
No warning. Your friend comes *flying over* the top of the closed
stall door. What do you think? Don't ask me. Ask my friend who
stood by the sink and watched me fly over the bathroom stall!
Long story short, it was my first encounter with the Almighty
Automatic Toilet. Li'l ol' innocent me was standing in the stall as
the toilet unexpectedly flushed itself, scaring me up the wall! I
know, I know… you had to be there.

My Guts

But what does this story have to do with these verses? No matter
how absurd our petitions seem, God hears us. He longs to comfort
us. So even today, as I sit on an automatic toilet and get weirded
out, God hears my cry. Taking it a step further, as you read through
these poems, you will see I depend on God greatly in every way.
As I go through life's occasional crises, I work through them by
writing poetry. As I bare my soul, you will experience my sorrows,
hopes, regrets, praises, encouragement, and passions…

Enjoy!

Crystal Joy

My Anchor

Empty inside,
       Just a shriveled soul that already died.
No ray of hope, not even a slice,
       And my gas tank is running on fumes
In this thing called life.

Take a hike, wise guy!
Excitement has arrived!

Unstoppable power! I'm bigger than life!
Uncontrolled energy?
       Is *that* what you're telling me?!
Believe me, there's nothing wrong,
Sometimes I just feel as brave as, well...King Kong!

I thought over 20 years of bipolar disorder
shipwrecked my life.
Looking back, it left me clinging to my Anchor, Jesus
Christ.
       Sometimes the waves still crash on me from
every direction,
But when I reflect on Jesus's death and resurrection
I know I can trust in His loving salvation.

Once again, now completely lost.
My life is uprooted, shaken up, and tossed.
Yes, Jesus, I do know You conquered death
on the Cross,
But right now, it just feels like another
inner holocaust.
So those times when I feel completely *off,*
May I remember Jesus, You bought my soul at
the steepest cost,
...Your life.

Philippians 4:13 KJV
I can do all things through Christ who strengthens me.

Ain't for Nothing

Friend, does the pain that grips you
　　　　Hold you hostage at a dead end?
　　　　Feel like there's no way out? Wait!
　　　　　　Jesus came to save, my friend!

　　　　　Your soul's sadness, anger, shackles,
　　　　　　imprisonment,
　　Are too heavy to cross this bridge to freedom.
Friend, God calls you to do one of the hardest
things ever
　　　　Offer Him your heart, your pain, and fully
　　　　surrender.

　　　　God didn't choose this pain
　　　　for you,
But if you let Him, He can certainly see you
through.

If through this pain, you were forced to get real with Jesus,
Examining if He's the real deal and can truly free us
        If this hurt eventually dropped you to your knees
      Crying out to Jesus as Savior, and finally finding
      true peace

If you could fathom the testimony of your
Godly healing,
      I tell you, dear Friend,
            This hurt ain't for
            nothing.

Revelation 21:4 NLT
     He will wipe every tear from their eyes, and there will be no more death or sorrow or crying or pain. All these things are gone forever.

Destined

I think this illness has **defeated** my voice
And someday I will abuse Your gift of FREE
CHOICE.
Is this an **unavoidable** ASSAULT?
Destined to take my life by default?

Jesus, I see what was meant to be

You were **destined** to be KILLED on that ol' ugly
tree!
Although *innocent*, You suffered for
EVERYBODY,
But the ONLY ONE *I care about* right now is,
well, me.

The **bloody lashes** on Your back are MINE
Meant to pay for my DESPICABLE CRIMES
But the only thing I am concerned with
Isn't Your passion, but regrettably mine.

Into the swine, Satan! Enough of your ENSNARING lies!

I now *turn my affection* back to my Savior,

Jesus Christ!

Yes, suffering is CERTAIN in this life,

But I'm <u>destined</u> to stand firm on the solid rock of CHRIST!

<u>Ephesians 5:17</u> NIV
Therefore do not be foolish, but understand what the will of the Lord is.

Dear Self,
The Cards You've Been Dealt

Know this, Self: Jesus can be your refuge in the storm.
The chains you struggle with will someday answer to the Lord.

He protects you day in and day out,
Fighting your battles, Self don't give up now!

Self, you can call on Jesus when things get tough,
But be fully genuine, don't let Satan call your bluff!

Dear Self, God is more powerful than the cards you've been dealt;
So run to Him for shelter, you'll find inner peace you've never felt.

<u>Psalm 32:7</u> ESV
You are a hiding place for me;
you preserve me from trouble;
you surround me with shouts of deliverance.

The Gospel in a Nutshell

When I was 15, Jesus tossed my life upside down. It was exhilarating! I was a total disgrace, but Jesus saved me just in time. I don't want anyone to stumble down that broken road as I did. I am proof that He has come for the sinners!

<u>**John 3:16-17**</u>

"For God so loved the world, He gave His one and only Son that whoever believes in Him shall not perish but have eternal life. <u>For God did not send His Son into the world to condemn the world, but to save the world through Him.</u>"

So, this is what I know to be true.

The key is to believe Jesus, the Son of God, died and rose again for you. Wearing your sins on the cross while He (the perfect Savior) died and rose back to life in your place. And when you ask for mercy, He gladly rushes to you and all of Heaven rejoices! My friend, Jesus wants you just as you are. He wants your damaged junk and all. You can't fix yourself. So why not give Jesus a try? He knows you better than you know yourself! And guess what! He's still wild about you!

With faith (belief), just watch what a Best Friend Jesus can be! Remember, it's a journey. He only takes what you give. He will never force Himself on you and never deny a seeking heart. Keep in mind that true faith leads to a desire to follow Him. Don't let Satan call your bluff!

<u>Romans 10:9</u> NIV
If you declare with your mouth, "Jesus is Lord," and believe in your heart that God raised him from the dead, you will be saved.

Here I Am

Yes, believing I can trust in my works is so terrifyingly
brazen.
Just horrified to mess up and lose my salvation.
Confidence in Your Blood, Lord isn't always roses and daisies,
And lately, my spiritual crawl has grown way too hazy.

Maybe You can give me a few pointers, God,
On how to stop being such a two-faced fraud.
I know Your forgiveness is profoundly beautiful,
But I believe the lie that my faith isn't suitable.

Perhaps I'm struggling to outdo Jesus's grace
When all I'm doing is spitting in His face.
I know His Blood has bought my freedom
Yet beyond my gratitude, He sees my treason.

Yes! I beg You, my dear Jesus Christ,
Don't let me lose sight of You in this spiritual plight!
You see, I've accepted Satan's lies for oh, so long!
I've got Your truths mixed up, backwards, and just all
wrong!

Jesus, Son of God, reveal Yourself to me.
You assure me Your salvation is entirely free.
You offer everything I need, just asking for faith
In Your Sonship, Lordship, and soul-saving grace.

So Jesus, although at times I don't fully understand,
Here I am.

John 14:6 NIV
Jesus answered, "I am the way and the truth and the life. ... No one comes to the Father except through me."

The Hypocrite's Cry

Lord, I bow to You with a hypocrite's lowly
heart;
 A follower who has now earned the
 name—Traitor.
 I deserted You amidst the commotion of
 the world,
And I am certainly not fit to call You my Lord.

 Forgive me, Jesus
Let the Crimson flow.
 Pour Your mercies over me.
 My Jesus, flood my soul!

Jesus, with all this sin I harbored within,
 You said you wouldn't give up on me still;
 You even said I am the salt of the earth,
 Yes, a city on a hill.

 Your compassion bewilders me;
 Your mercies run rampant on that
 ol' ugly tree.
My Jesus, Your wounds and Your
stripes
 Forever set me free!

Lord, because of Your mercy,
I bow to You with a servant's forgiven and
eager heart.

Crimson Stains

Hard to trust in Jesus's grace
When my soul is nothing but
a sinful waste.
Digging deeper and deeper, just seems like
a game
Approaching the point where I'm suffocating in
shame.

Oh, why? Oh *why*, dear God, did You
die for me?
I have brought You nothing, can't
You see?!
No Lord! Cast Satan and his puppets into the
swine!
I refuse to remain spiritually blind!

Jesus, You know the depth of my sins,
But Your crimson stains overpower them!
Your mercies flooded crimson on that ol' ugly Cross;
Yes precious Jesus, You paid the ultimate cost!

For way too long I have been Your long-lost
sheep.
Paranoid of Satan and his terrifying
fleet.
Needed serious refuge, I was going
insane;
But You love me enough to wash me in
Your crimson stains!

Jesus, my Substitute, oh how I long to come
Home!
So I can sing Your praises as I bow before Your
Throne.

1 Peter 2:24 NLT
He personally carried our sins in his body on the cross
so that we can be dead to sin and live for what is right.
By his wounds you are healed.

When I Close my Eyes

My knees tremble in the glory of
Your Presence;
Precious Majesty, I come to honor
You now.
Hear my praises exalt You from my innermost being,
While I worship You from the
depths of my soul.

When I close my eyes,
I see Your Perfection standing before me.
Your Holy Word is a love letter
Speaking intimately to my spirit,
Luring me and tempting me for more.

My devoted Jesus, Your love for me is so real.
So raw.
So here, dear Lord, at Your feet I
fall.
Strip search my spirit, O God!
Destroy all that is not
of You
And chuck it to the hogs!

Jesus, You have shown me what true love is,
A bond that can never be more intimate
Than between the Savior and His 'beloved'.

I invite You to be my love...my passion...my life...
My everything...

John 14:21 ESV
Whoever has my commandments and keeps them,
he it is who loves me.
And he who loves me will be loved by my Father,
and I will love him and manifest myself to him.

My friend Dave grieves his son Isaac, who committed suicide in 2001. (Names changed.)

Love Story

Dave, the moment you held baby Isaac in your hands,
The birth of a never-ending, father-son love story began.
Situations change, but the love always remains,
And the passion you hold for him
Is still as strong as it's ever been.

God knows the pain cuts so incredibly deep, my friend,
But did you know love stories never have to end?
Rekindle the memories, the photos, any reminders of his life—
Share stories of Isaac! Keep his memory alive!

Dave, the moment you trusted in Jesus's nail-scarred hands,
Your journey in a never-ending, Father-son love story began.
Situations change, but His love always remains,
And the passion He holds for you will always stand,
As He holds your broken heart by the Blood of the Lamb.

Nobody can *ever* undo Jesus's Bloody Stripes.

Nobody can *ever* limit the love of Jesus Christ.

So no Dave, nobody can *ever* force you to give up your fight.

Because nobody can *ever* snuff out Isaac's light.

Romans 8:37-39 ESV
No, in all these things we are more than conquerors through him who loved us. For I am sure that neither death nor life, nor angels nor rulers, nor things present nor things to come, nor powers, nor height nor depth, nor anything else in all creation, will be able to separate us from the love of God in Christ Jesus our Lord.

Whoops!

Looks Like You Gotta Wait and See!

My Scrambled Heart

Finding Hope Amongst the Hopelessness

Chapter 2
My Scrambled Heart: Finding Hope Amongst the
Hopelessness

"Stuff 'n' Things"

Psalm 9:9-10 NLT
The LORD is a **shelter** for the OPPRESSED,

a refuge in times of trouble.

Those who know your name trust

in **You,**

for you, **O LORD, do not abandon**
those who

search for You.

My Guts
As you read through this heart-wrenching chapter in my poetry,
you will find an imperfect person who sometimes feels broken.
However, other times I let God move in unexpected, beautiful
ways. You will see that I have become untrustful and downright
angry at God. Still, He never fails to reveal His loving patience. I'm
learning He truly is my refuge. It's comforting to know that when
we seek Him, He's got open arms—always. Praise God!

Q: Do you especially feel God's presence in certain areas of your
life? Praise Him! Are there areas that could be improved? Trust His
Word, He will never forsake those who seek Him!

Dare Ya!

Take a moment and examine your spirit. Are you right with God? If not, would you like to be? God knows your heart. When you're ready, open up to Him. Tell Him about your hurt. Your anger. Your shame. Your needs. Your desires. Your hopes. Anything! Yes, your dreams and aspirations! He cares about every little speck of your life.

Hopefully Someday

If there's anything I am gradually forgetting in life,
It's the true healing I can find in Jesus Christ.
Despite all my anger, sin, sadness, and pain,
I must remember Jesus sees beyond my shame.

Those times when chaos and despair barge in,
I refuse to let God heal my heart again.
He still offers to be a faithful, never-ending Friend,
Even though He knows my rage is directed at Him.

Through His tears, Jesus doesn't condemn me,
Just continues to miss me; continues to love me.
Even when I turn my back on Him,
Sadly yes; time and again.

I know any day could be too late,
Forgetting I'm gambling with my ultimate fate.
I know this God I continue to hurt
Holds my destiny of which I flirt.

I scream, "How could this God of love
judge *me*?!
He doesn't know *half* of my misery!"

But I'm reminded, quite the contrary.
Jesus *chose* to give His *all* for me.
He died for my soul, brutally nailed to a tree,
To *become* my healing and set me free.

Hopefully someday I can relinquish my anger.
Hopefully someday the pain won't so strongly linger.
Hopefully someday I will begin to trust in You.
Hopefully someday You'll see me through.

Hopefully someday. I will let You *become* my hope.
Yes. Hopefully someday...

Psalm 39:7 NIV
But now, Lord, what do I look for? My hope is in you.

God Understands

Your rainstorms beckon me,
Hiding private tears only You can see.
So for You, Jesus, I drop to my knees.
My Lord, hear my prayer please.

Jesus, You found me drowning in anger,
But with loving empathy, You knew I needed a Savior.
No, You didn't abandon me to the grave,
You pursued me as Your own to save.

Jesus, that Holy night You invited me in,
You knew how much anger I still harbored within.
Too deep-rooted to simply release
Far too long I've felt like an evil beast.

But something changed today.

I learned Your Cross has the final say—
So I glorify You, Jesus! My slaughtered Lamb!
Your Sacrifice freed my shame with two words—

"God understands."

Psalm 106:1 NIV
Praise the LORD. Give thanks to the LORD,
for he is good; his love endures forever.

The Broken Poem

So terrified in my sin You'll surely abandon me
But when the Hebrews lost their faith,
In Your love, You still parted the Red Sea.

I'm fully trampled and broken,
But *You*, my Deliverer, have spoken.
Yes. Your Blood still calls me by name—
For it was You, for me, who was horrifically slain.

You assure me regardless of how I feel,
I will always find shelter within Your Spirit's
seal,
So my soul that You redeemed on the cross—
The powers of darkness can never steal.

Romans 8:18 NIV
**I consider that our present sufferings are not worth
comparing with the glory that will be revealed in us.**

Dear Self,
When Your Life Is Crumbling...

Dear Self, although God's healing may feel delayed at times,
> I do know He longs to quiet your desperate cries...

I just pray, Dear Self, that when your life is crumbling,
You hang tight to Jesus before you start stumbling.

> Yes, despite the brokenness, You are still His.
> So please, Self, never lose sight of who your God is...

...God is your **HOPE.** Sacrifice. Comforter. **Soul Mate.**
Redeemer. Healer. **Lover of your soul**. Refuge.
> Deliverer. Protector.
Risen Savior. Best Friend...
> ***Yours***...Always and forever.

2 Corinthians 1:5 ESV
For the more we suffer for Christ,
the more God will shower us with his comfort through Christ.

The Tears of my Soul

The tears of my soul
Hidden and unseen
MASKED by laughter
And good spirits—
Alone in my screams.

Cannot express myself
My reality rots in the
Realm of the unknown.
Behind dry eyes lives the violent river
Of the tearful brimming soul—

I retreat within and find
Heartache and misery
But not for your eyes
Tucked too deep inside—

No matter how intense the
pain
The waters NEVER rupture the
flood gates
You will NEVER see the tears of my soul.

Just dry eyes
      MASKED by laughter
And good spirits
         Only for you.

Psalm 126:5 NLT
Those who plant in tears
      will harvest with shouts of joy.

Keep Healing Me, Jesus

Your Hand is mighty,
Mighty to reach the sick
And the lame.

You carry the weak,
The sorrowful,
And You feel all our pain.

Keep healing me Jesus,
In the only way You can do.
You are so moved by my
hurt,
I see all Your tears too—

The same strong Hands
Who conquered death on the Cross
Are the same tender Hands
That hold me when I'm at a loss.

It is You who loved me first
With Your Blood and Your Stripes
I know I can carry on—
But only with You by my side.

Keep healing me Jesus,
When life seems in disarray,
Please walk with me, talk with me,
Every night, every day.

I refuse to admit defeat!
I am sure You will see me
through!
You will restore my broken
spirit,
Lord, may I only trust in You!

<u>1 Chronicles 16:11</u> NKJV
Seek the L<small>ORD</small> and His strength; Seek His face evermore!

Hold On

I do know You cherish my life,
Otherwise, for me, You wouldn't have died.
My precious Jesus nailed to a tree,
How could I question Your love for me?

Jesus, help me to hold on to Your
healing—
No matter how long I am called to remain
hurting.
Still want to go to my Heavenly
Home now,
—That much is true—

But all I will say is, let my pain somehow glorify You.

<u>Micah 7:7</u> **NKJV**
Therefore I will look to the LORD;
I will wait for the God of my salvation;
My God will hear me.

Dear Self,
No Pressure...

Self, when you're in a funk, focus on what you
treasure most.
Your pets, your favorite person, the Holy
Ghost?

Dear Self, when you're lonely, you can pick up God's
Word
Or sing His praises, get your spirit stirred!

I know Dear Self, at times it's hard to
do anything
Even when you're in the presence of God
your King.

No, Dear Self, some people just might not
get it,
No pressure, sometimes all you can do is collect
your head and sit.

Matthew 11:28-30 NIV
**Come to me, all you who are weary and burdened, and
I will give you rest. Take my yoke upon you and learn from me, for
I am gentle and humble in heart, and you will find rest for your
souls. For my yoke is easy and my burden is light.**

Broken Within

I am broken within
Shattered to pieces
Empty inside
Can't find my sweet Jesus—

Where is this Lord
That I call my own?
So Holy, so Sacred
He is all that I know.

As the clouds roll in
And the sun falls dim
My soul lives in torment
As I wait for Him.

Struggling to escape
The images of my death,
Don't want to die,
But can't catch my own breath—

I am broken within,
Shattered to pieces,
Empty inside—
Still my hope rests in Jesus!

Psalm 34:18 NIV
The Lord is close to the brokenhearted
and saves those who are crushed in spirit.

Note to Self

Jesus already claimed defeat
Over all that Satan will throw at me.
No more need for me to be afraid,
God is my Reeboks in this race.

Deuteronomy 31:8 NIV
The LORD himself goes before you and will be with you;
he will never leave you nor forsake you.
Do not be afraid; do not be discouraged.

Journey of Grief

Can't force this mass out of my throat.
Satan is butchering my last remnant of hope.
Where is this journey of grief headed?
This intense pain is just too deeply embedded—

My soul almost succumbs to the violent waves.
Wildly tossing me, stealing my praise—
Where is this journey of grief headed?
"Don't give up..." Yes, I know Who said it—

Yet still convinced Satan will soon win,
Now I see I'm in grave condition—
Where is this journey of grief headed?
To a place of horror? My soul's most dreaded?---

Nope, straight to You, Jesus—

Sometimes calling on You, Lord
Feels so useless in this chaotic world,
So with limited faith
I ask You to wipe clean my slate.

Yes, I come to You, Jesus,
The Expert at reviving
wrecked spirits
And understanding damaged praise.

Psalm 51:10 **NLT**
Create in me a clean heart, O God.
Renew a loyal spirit within me.

Extra Close to Me

Jesus, no matter how bad it hurts,
    When my life just feels cursed,
  Grant me the passion to serve You still
As I cautiously welcome Your divine will.

    So, dear Lord, those times I face
  The worst that worst can be,
    May You never cease to remind
    me, Lord,
      You are extra close to me

      as I grieve.

1 Thessalonians 4:13 NLT
And now, dear brothers and sisters,
    we want you to know what will happen to the believers
      who have died so you will not grieve like people who
      have no hope.

Haunted

Your pitiful lies mask your corrupt heart—
Guilt? No! Your spirit thrives in the dark!
Why must you hide?
You're destroying her from within!
Don't you even see your own dreadful sin?

But no, your crimes have overcome,
Speak no more with your deceitful tongue!
You shout blame at your accuser,
Using shame and falsehood to oppress her!

In you, she becomes a total disgrace
Trapped in her anger, until it's all she can
taste—
She harbors your truth from deep within,
Forced to pretend she isn't haunted by
your sin.

<u>Colossians 3:12-13</u> NKJV
**Therefore, as *the* elect of God, holy and beloved, put on tender
mercies, kindness, humility, meekness, longsuffering; bearing with
one another, and forgiving one another, if anyone has a complaint
against another; even as Christ forgave you, so you also *must do.***

Camouflaged Tears

Yes, she's experienced the love of her Savior,
But sometimes she feels He's just been a traitor—
Forsaking her in the worst way ever,
Without the Divine love to make things better.

Laughter and smiles to mask the horror,
Living a lie to hide the cards that were dealt her,
Unable to escape her own fierce anger,
Forced to walk a life of paranoia and danger.

At times, she has challenged God's authority in this
world,
Yet sometimes she's still able to reach out to Him as
her Lord.
Not once has He turned her away—
He just offers, *"My love, welcome...repent and have
faith."*

However, her inner anguish never seems to cease.
She desperately begs God to be her long-awaited peace,
Longing for the healing she knows only comes from Him,
As her camouflaged tears relentlessly flood over the brim.

Psalm 32:7 NIV
You are my hiding place;
You will protect me from trouble
and surround me with songs of deliverance.

One

My God, as I gave You my everything,
I asked You to break me at Your altar.
So as You sit with me through this brokenness—
I know I will soon find Oneness in You, my Father.

The torment seizing my soul today
Will certainly not prevail.
Satan's attempts at defeating me
Will someday answer to Your Nails.

Precious Lord, never *ever* hesitate,
Each moment I begin to stray,
DROP me to my knees!
Yes—break my soul anew,
Until my one and only passion
Is to forever be One with You.

Psalm 71:8 NIV
**My mouth is filled with your praise,
declaring your splendor all day long.**

The Band Marches On

Obsessed with the demons
That demand her soul
Willing to do anything to be left alone
But the band marches on
As she remains Satan's foolish pawn

Terror pumps through her veins
Living with a broken heart
And a damaged brain
Nowhere to retreat
Already going insane—

Yes, without a care
The band marches on
And Satan still thinks
She's his foolish pawn—

But no!
Jesus gave her new life!
And Satan falls shaking
At the sight of Jesus Christ!

1 Peter 5:8 ESV
Be sober, be vigilant;
because your adversary the devil
walks about like a roaring lion,
seeking whom he may devour.

Victorious Crimson

Jesus, when the tears begin to fall
And my faith has hit a wall,
Or when I feel like I just don't matter—
I know You are fully saddened by
the reality, God,
That sometimes my whole self feels shattered.

In You, I still hope for some sort of relief;
May I soon learn to run to You for desperate retreat.
Yes, Your death has conquered all with such
victorious Crimson—
And for me, my Lord, You have most certainly risen!

Precious Jesus, how can I not give You my life?
You lived, died, and rose for me,
my dear Jesus Christ!
The story is not over! You walk with
me day by day!
Steadily molding me into a masterpiece from
ordinary clay.

Psalm 91:14-15 NIV
"Because he loves me," says the LORD, "I will rescue him;
I will protect him, for he acknowledges my name.
He will call on me, and I will answer him;
I will be with him in trouble,
I will deliver him and honor him."

Baby Steps

Grew too blind to see who You truly are,
Blaming You, precious Jesus, yes I took it too far.
I do want to fully give You my life and surrender my soul,
But abandoning this anger would demand such a great toll—

Precious Jesus, You are the Way, the Truth, and the Life,
For my sins, Lord, You paid the ultimate price!
All this time I thought You had ill-intent up Your sleeve.
But You're the One who hung on that cross, not me!

Your everlasting love and mercy abound!
And for some peculiar reason, You'll grant me a
crown—
I celebrate the glorious night we first met,
But just for now, my Jesus, let's return to baby steps.

Psalm 103:8 NKJV
The Lord *is* merciful and gracious,
Slow to anger, and abounding in mercy.

Finding Beauty in the Brokenness

Many times I just feel hate,
Or I hurt so bad, I don't care to pray.
But I know this is not Your will, O Lord,
My soul belongs to You and is not of this world.

You call me to faith, You call me to trust,
In a way only a broken heart could
muster up.
I need my Jesus more than the average joe,
And I count my blessings, that I must depend on
Him so.

Jesus and I have a special kind of
relationship,
Slowly and tenderly, bit by bit—
He meets me where I am in this brokenness,
Healing the hole in my heart and restoring
my spirit.

Finding the beauty in my brokenness is not
easy to do,
But I have found Jesus waiting there to
see me through—

And it's enough to help me gradually trust
in Him,

As each day starts over—
again and again.

Psalm 9:10 NIV
Those who know your name trust in you,

for you, LORD, have never forsaken those who seek you.

Lies

Satan tells me if I follow him, he will soothe my cries,
But no, for my salvation, Jesus gave up His own life!
Satan believes he has eternally shackled my soul,
Fooling me to hide my light under a bowl—

When the hurt is so severe that my heart begins to roam,
And I believe it's *my* choice of when to go Home,
I find I've been blinded by Satan's lies—
Nearly bankrupting my soul—yes, I was very unwise.

I stomp on Satan and mock his wicked lies!
Because You, dear Jesus have given me new life!
So not this time, Satan! I'm washed in the Blood!
My faith resides solely with Jesus's Crimson flood!

<u>John 8:44</u> NIV
...[Satan] was a murderer from the beginning, not holding to the truth,
for there is no truth in him. When he lies, he speaks his native language,
for he is a liar and the father of lies.

The Demons Within

Is this a game from the demons within?
Emotions run rampant, while hopelessness settles in,
This anguish inside me is finally seizing control.
Can these demons fatally steal my soul?

Satan is fervently digging my grave,
But no, the Son of God already calls me saved—
Yes, of course I still long for Jesus's healing!
But at times my prayers seem to bounce off the
ceiling.

Should I raise the white flag and admit defeat?
By no means! Jesus calls me to kneel at His feet!
My faith says Jesus will see me through,
Come, my friend, He longs to rescue you too—

Deuteronomy 31:6 NKJV
Be strong and of good courage,
do not fear nor be afraid of them;
for the LORD your God,
He *is* the One who goes with you.
He will not leave you nor forsake you."

Dear Self, You Have Hope

Dear Self, your woes may feel like many,
But remember! Your blessings are plenty!

When you feel like giving in,
Remember, Jesus already made
the win!

Satan has been crushed under His feet,
And Jesus will soon jack up the heat!

Dear Self, don't succumb to this sin,
Your dearest blessings are life and hope in Him.

Isaiah 40:31 NKJV
But those who wait on the LORD
Shall renew *their* strength;
They shall mount up with wings like eagles,
They shall run and not be weary,
They shall walk and not faint.

Leave Them to Die

Closing my eyes, I leave them to die,
Knowing I should be leading them to Christ.
As I judge a world consumed by hate
Satan laughs as I gulp down his most appetizing bait.

Snubbing the lost,
Overlooking the cross.
Am I wasting Jesus's Blood?
Holding back on His undying love?

Thought His Blood wasn't potent enough.
Perhaps His scars are not Superhero-tough?
Yes, the world must be too far gone,
Too twisted, polluted, and just all wrong.

When I look within,
I'm the one who has hoarded even *more* sin.
A *believer* clinging to a hateful heart,
Repulsively abandoning the lost—
To suffer and die in the dark.

Proverbs 11:2 NKJV
When pride comes, then comes shame;
But with the humble *is* wisdom.

Dear Self, What Do You Do?

Self, you see the lonely widow,
Her heart and spirit growing so brittle—

Self, that addict mourning his own dignity—
Do you know today he eternally lost his victory?

The poor, the hurting—
Self, these are the people for whom Jesus died!

He calls us to love unconditionally,
So love with no end in sight!

So Self, what do you do?
Show Jesus's love to all people, not just a select few!

1 John 3:17 NKJV
But whoever has this world's goods,
and sees his brother in need,
and shuts up his heart from him,
how does the love of God abide in him?

Knees

You called me "Yours" before I knew You;
You called me "child" before I came to be;
You called me "loved" before I loved You;
Your mercy drops me to my knees.

You love me unconditionally—
Better than the world could ever offer me!
Yes, You opened my eyes!
By Your compassion, You grant me forever life.

I called You, "Glorious" when I first saw You;
I called You, "Savior" when You set me free;
I called You, "Son of God" as You taught me Your truths;
Yes, Your presence just drops me to my knees.

1 John 4:19 NIV
We love because he first loved us.

When Free Isn't Free

Wish it was how it used to be,
Free to drink and free to be me.
Messing up when nothing mattered
'Til I drank too much and my friends
all scattered...

Made my own rules
Drunk or hungover at school,
Yes, people could see, as they
laughed at me.
Maybe drinking wasn't all it was
cracked up to be.

When my drunken world leaves me sick as
can be,
And I promise myself that was my last
drink...
Twenty-five years later, I still feel the need
And realize drinking back then I was never
really free.

When my mind restores from its blackened
oblivion...
And the bottle continues to ruin the fun,
I will still tell you I need some vodka or rum,
And accept the fact that Satan won...
...Again

Galatians 5:1 NIV
It is for freedom that Christ has set us free.
Stand firm, then, and do not let yourselves
be burdened again by a yoke of slavery.

The Bottle

Devoured from *within*,
My FAITH falls dim...
Need to trust in my Savior,
But keep *putting Him off* until
LATER...

No matter how many *YEARS* go by,
Or how hard I TRY,
The BOTTLE always SNEAKS back in...
Sporting its own *evil grin.*

Will I *ever* be free?!
Dear God! HELP me, please!
I see my own *devilish sin...*
Has got me in TROUBLE *again...*

2 Thessalonians 3:3 ESV
But the Lord is faithful. He will establish you
and guard you against the evil one.

Was...

I was the criminal—drowning in sin.
I was the addict—yes, losing my friends.
I was the hopeless—thought it best just to die.
I was the mourning—but nobody saw my cry.
I was the tempted—a sheep led astray.
I was the faithless—but no, not today—

**—Because when I was the lost,
Jesus showed me the Way!**

Jesus, loving Son of God,
Have mercy on the criminal!
Win victory for the addict!
Be the hope for the hopeless!
Lavish comfort on the mourning!
Be the strength for the tempted—
Give faith to the faithless—

**And continue to lovingly fight for
The salvation of the lost.**

Psalm 86:5 ESV
**For you, O Lord, are good and forgiving,
abounding in steadfast love to all who call upon you.**

Joke's on You

They say I've gone mad
Yes, my specialty—

Last to find out
Mental drought.
Guess the joke's on me
Cuz that's all they see—

Living my life in vain
I'm nothing but insane,
Just the brunt of jokes
Is my brain just a hoax?

Nope, but I can assure ya—
Those goats standing on my car
"Meowed" all the way to the bar.
But the bald one who smelled of lemon
Was snatched by a famished gremlin—

Okay, so maybe I'm a tidbit odd,
But I can still live my life to glorify God!

1 Corinthians 10:31 NLT
So whether you eat or drink,
or whatever you do,
do it all for the glory of God.

You Will Carry Me On

Jesus, I can't see You right now
But I will somehow follow You,
Because my blind faith says
You are guiding me safely through
These exhausting waters—

Jesus, I can't sense You right now,
But as You lead, I will trust in You,
Because my hopeful faith says,
Only You can eradicate all
The sorrow I cling to—

My Savior, I can't touch You right now,
But I will tearfully praise You,
Because my humble faith says
Your pierced hands have written my name
In Your Lamb's Book of Life.

Jesus—
In times like these
When my tears drown my sinking heart,
You will always be my Savior—
Yes, my Super Hero.

You will carry me on,
And I will always be okay.
I am exclusively Yours,
And You are abundantly mine.
All I need is in You.

Revelation 21:4 NLT
He will wipe every tear from their eyes,
and there will be no more death or sorrow or crying or pain.
All these things are gone forever.

Taboo Files
&

"Dear Self"
Commentaries

Chapter 3
Taboo Files & "Dear Self" Commentaries

"Stuff 'n' Things"

1 John 4:4 NKJV

You are from God, **little children,**
and have **overcome them,** because
He who is **in you**
is greater than he who is in the world.

Q: Ever feel like the struggles you're desperately trying to swim from just drag you deeper into the rip current? Perhaps you or someone you know is ready to raise the white flag and surrender? Simply fed up? You have hope...

My Guts: Sometimes, I get lost in my misery. Defeated. But I realize no matter how I feel, in Christ, I will always be a conqueror! An overcomer. I refuse to let Satan define me. As believers in Jesus, the hurdles we must jump - or frequently trip over - cannot consume us. Even if by death. Yes, this verse screams hope! The God of the universe is *inside* us! I know who I belong to - the biggest, baddest Conqueror of all time! The One who died a torturous death and bought my soul on that ugly cross. And was risen to life on the third day! Imagine that! I know where I belong! Do you? Believers will someday be at Home with Jesus! Hallelujah! And nobody can take that away. Not even the worst pain or the darkest powers of this world! My friend, whatever you are going through, Jesus is offering you something better. Do you believe?

Instincts

Sometimes I can hide the fact
That my life is falling apart
Just You alone Lord, see the days
When my tears drown my heart.

At times I can bury this monster
So deep down inside,
Thinking if I honestly searched
There would be no horror to find.

Again, my instincts suddenly creep up
Without the courtesy of warning,
Shamefully reminding me of those
Who would be left behind mourning…

Don't get me wrong.
I've asked Jesus to be my salvation.
Yes, we can always call on Him
In these times of desperation.

Psalm 55:22 NKJV
Cast your burden on the Lord,
And He shall sustain you;
He shall never permit the righteous to be moved.

Dear Self,
You Have a Mission

As miniscule as you may feel at times,
Jesus is holding you in His nail-scarred hands.

The way you feel right now may block your
spiritual vision,
But Jesus truly does hold for you a beautiful,
meaningful mission.

Dear Self, when you offer your desperation to the
Lord,
He can transform it into something majestically more!

His plans for you will transcend all your
expectations!
So in your misery Dear Self, cling to
His patience.

Isaiah 41:13 NIV
For I am the LORD your God
who takes hold of your right hand
and says to you, "Do not fear;
I will help you."

Tomb

Spiraling into depression
    Refusing resuscitation.
Let the blackness consume
      Anticipating my tomb.

Need to escape this world
    No, perhaps I need to chat
    with my Lord—

Spiraling into depression,
Yes, Jesus is my salvation.
He saved me from utter doom
    When He walked right outta that tomb.

1 Peter 1:3 NIV
Praise be to the God and Father of our Lord Jesus Christ!
In his great mercy he has given us new birth
into a living hope through the
resurrection of Jesus Christ from the dead,

Dear Self,
There's Power in the Blood

Dear Self, I know at times you may feel
totally lost,
> But try to remember, there's
> power in the Cross.

Scripture says the battle has already
been won,
Even when the mound on your shoulders
weighs over a ton.

> No Dear Self, this pain won't last
> forever,
> Keep that in mind as your soul feels
> bound and tethered.

Satan is not strong enough to steal your life—
There is too much power in the Blood of Christ!
Yes, enough to defeat Satan and win this fight.

2 Chronicles 32:8 NKJV
With him *is* an arm of flesh;
but with us *is* the LORD our God,
to help us and to fight our battles.

Stricken

The sting of hate consumes me from within,
Lingering in a wake of a host of sin—
So mad at God, "Where have You been??!"
Forcing me to face utter terror time and again!

I am fully angry with You, Lord!
You left me for dead in this world—
Does "free will" really sound fair
When a child is stricken beyond repair?!

You say, "Blessed are the poor in spirit,"
But I just don't know if I'm ready to hear it
You say, "Blessed are those who mourn,"
But Lord, my being is just too dreadfully torn!

Jesus, I know You begged to be spared from *my* Cross!
And terrified, You paid the sin-debt for me, the lost.
You bore the punishment of all my hate, anger, and sin—
Casting them in the fire, only for me to dig them up again.

Even still, I don't doubt You can truly set me free
You say all I need is faith as little as a mustard seed.
Oh, my Lord, may I soon be able to cling to You
When my inner being is finally willing to be renewed.

Ephesians 4:27 ESV
And give no opportunity to the devil.

Dear Self, He Will Listen

Dear Self, You will never find true peace in
this world.
> So instead, offer up your
> heartache to the Lord.

> God alone knows your pain better
> than you do.
So Dear Self, never second guess Jesus's love
for you.

> Spill your guts to your Savior, Self. Yes, He will
> listen.
He sees your tears and longs to carry your burdens.

Grasp this, Self! No problem is too big for Jesus our Lord!
> Because of His Sacrifice, Jesus has overcome the
> world!

John 16:33 NIV
I have told you these things,
> **so that in me you may have peace.**
In this world you will have trouble.
> **But take heart! I have overcome the world.**

Invasive Thoughts

I grieve for my soul—
Satan's grip has a tremendous hold.
Feels like just yesterday I was fully my Lord's,
But now I've been trampled in this spiritual war.

Am I really forever lost?
Satan's voice *screams* into my invasive thoughts!
My mind frantically spins trying to regain control,
But Satan laughs. It's my free will that he stole—

Forsaking this life as it demands a dead end—
Sudden death. My new best friend?
Don't have a clue how to beat this fight.
Feels like the only thing I can do is lie down and die.

No! Father God, the evil overpowering my brain
I give fully to You, in Jesus's Holy Name!

Job 28:28 NIV
And he said to the human race,
"The fear of the Lord—that is wisdom,
and to shun evil is understanding.

Dear Self,
Hold Out

When you feel too messed up and you just want to die,
Remember, Dear Self, you're believing Satan's lies.

Dear Self, there's no hope in self-inflicted death,
Just sorrowful pain and a soul plagued with regrets.

Right now you don't see it, but God has a plan!
You won't always be sinking in sifting sand.

I dare you, Dear Self! Just wait and see!
Hold out a bit longer and let Christ set you free!

<u>Galatians 6:9</u> **NLT**
So let's not get tired of doing what is good.
At just the right time we will reap a harvest of blessing
if we don't give up.

Your Perfect Time

Just want to close my eyes, Lord—
And leave this dreadful world,
Hope that's my brain entertaining a lie,
Knowing I'm not ready to say "goodbye—"

God, Your healing will come at Your
perfect time.
So, however difficult for me to try,
I raise my hands and lift Your Name
on high—
Even when I just want to shut down and cry.

Job 5:11 NKJV
He sets on high those who are lowly,
And those who mourn are lifted to safety.

Dear Self,
Don't You Dare Surrender!

Dear Self, are you trapped in a rut, ready to give in?
Fight with all your strength! This isn't
the end!

**Yes Self, this world rages onward in
demonic hate
But it's not your time for those
Pearly Gates—**

**Ask God for help, mercy, and strength,
And glorify Him with much heartfelt
praise—**

Self, have you not heard?
We combat Satan with God's Holy Word!

Yes! Absorb those Scriptures into your inner core!
Self, don't you dare surrender to this
spiritual war!

James 1:12 NLT
God blesses those who patiently endure testing and temptation.
Afterward they will receive the crown of life that God
has promised to those who love him.

The Good News:

The Knocking Door

Chapter 4
The Good News: The Knocking Door

"Stuff 'n' Things"

<u>Ephesians 2:8-9</u> NIV

For it is by **grace** you have been saved, through **faith**—
and this is **not from yourselves,**
it is the **gift of God**—
not by works, so that **no one** can boast.

<u>Check This Out!</u>

I was the teen known for the vodka in my closet, the loose morals that accompanied it, and many more things I don't care to say. But I knew there was a God. I've been to church. I was a-ok, right? My 11th-grade classmate offers, "My boyfriend is an evangelist, do you want to hear his cassette tape?" *Great. This is all I need. Something else to do...*

I politely agreed and took it home. A week later, I finally listened to it to pacify her. Then it happened: That fateful night on October 27, 1994. To my surprise, God had a plan! He set my soul on FIRE! I had never felt so alive! I finally met the love of my life!!! I was star-struck, and when I asked Him, this newfound Jesus immediately stripped all the sin from my spirit and washed me in His Blood! How could I not accept Him as my Lord and Savior? That's it! I was in *loooove!* At that exact moment, the mess I made of my life? Jesus's Blood erased my blame. I was pure. Forgiven. And He gradually changed me into who I am today. Still working, though! No, not nearly perfect.

But if I died one second after accepting Jesus as my Savior, I would surely be in heaven. That's what this verse means. I'll never be able to earn it. I know my soul is safe because it's all about faith! Are you safe?

<u>My Guts</u>

Not everybody has such a big experience when first meeting Jesus. The most important thing would be maintaining that "fire" throughout our walk with Him daily. And I'll be the first to be honest and say I need to crawl back to God's throne and beg for His mercy. Yes. I lost my First Love. My Jesus. As my soul is being convicted of this at this present moment, I have decided to go to Him in deep prayer tonight. For those of you who are so close to God, and His Spirit is pouring out of you, I praise Him for your walk so truly! But if you're not, I want to assure you, friend, God will never turn away a seeking heart. Not there yet? I get it. If you need, simply ask Him for spiritual thirst. If you mean it, God will come to you. I want that for you, my friend.

Third Day

Dear Jesus, You remind me of why You were slain—
We can't save ourselves—so You wore all our blame.
Terrified, You poured out Your Blood and died on the Cross—
And You reach out to us sinners because You came for the lost!

On the third day Jesus, You were risen!
You defeated the shackles of death and Satan!
Now upon faith, You lovingly welcome us in—
Such a celebration when we choose You over sin!

John 5:28-29 NIV
Do not be amazed at this, for a time is coming when all who are in their graves will hear his voice and come out—those who have done what is good will rise to live, and those who have done what is evil will rise to be condemned.

Concerned? That's ok. Read on—

John 1:12 NIV
Yet to all who did receive him, to those who believed in his name, he gave the right to become children of God—

Forgiveness. Amazing, huh?

Crimson Flood

Your love beckons me to Your Kingdom,
A holy love I will never fully fathom.
My Jesus, I bow in awe of Your glory!
For me, You held back on Your fury,
Yes, You let Your Crimson Flood flow—

You call repentant criminals Your children.
A holy love I will never fully fathom.
Mercy is made possible only by You, Jesus.
For all us outlaws, You died just to free us.
Yes, You let Your Crimson Flood flow—

You own the keys to that evil dungeon.
A holy love I will never fathom.
You saved our souls from that ol' ugly place.
We are dependent solely on Your grace.
Yes, You let Your Crimson Flood flow—

<u>1 John 1:7</u> **ESV**
But if we walk in the light, as he is in the light,
we have fellowship with one another,
and the blood of Jesus his Son cleanses us from all sin.

You Did Whaaaaat??

Jesus, You have a message. At first, nobody understood. Then the third day after You died, You walked straight outta that tomb! Frightening the masses! And You are alive in Heaven today!

Breaking Your Law separates us from You. But You refused to leave it that way! So You did the only thing possible to save our souls—

Son of God, You chose to die...*instead of us.* You *became* our sin. You took our punishment! Jesus, when we call out to You as Lord and Savior, the very Son of God, with belief in Your Sacrifice and resurrection, You see us believers as *blameless!* You bless us with a forever life that not one of us deserves!

With Your help, You call us to turn from our sin, and simply believe in You, Lord Jesus – the Son of God! Thank You for taking my punishment, Jesus. You died for me, so I will live for You. In Your Name, amen!

Matthew 7:21 NIV
Not everyone who says to me, 'Lord, Lord,' will enter the kingdom of heaven, but only the one who does the will of my Father who is in heaven.

It's All You, Jesus!

Jesus, when You showed me
You wanted to be my Sacrifice,
I was lost and filthy with sin.

But as I ask for mercy,
You always forgive me,
Time and time again.

Jesus, the Son of God—
It was You who paid the price,
Who purchased my life,
Savior, I long to serve only You!

It's all You, Jesus and
Your painful gift of love—
Oh, what a mess I'd be
If not washed in Your Blood!

I praise You, Jesus,
For Your infinite mercy and love—
Your acceptance, forgiveness
And of course Your passionate Blood!

John 15:13 NIV
Greater love has no one than this:
to lay down one's life for one's friends.

Divine Trade

To me, the gift of Your Blood is priceless,
A concept the lost consider senseless.
But no, this is a power that can never be matched!
From believers, Your Blood can never be snatched!

My Jesus, Your Blood means more than the world to me!
But You assure me, it's not priceless, it was never really free.
There was a huge price tag on my soul,
Your very life was sacrificed to make me whole.

My Lord, Jesus Christ, You suffered terribly!
How could I forget all that terrifying agony?
I praise You, my Lord, for the price You paid,
You died *instead* of me, what a Divine trade—

Romans 6:23 **ESV**
For the wages of sin is death, but the free gift
of God is eternal life in Christ Jesus our Lord.

Dear Self,
Kneel in Awe

Loving, precious Lord. Yes! I open the door!
Dear Self, it's okay if you drop to the floor—

Son of God! My sins are many!
But You show me that faith in
You is plenty.

Dear Self, now confess your sins
Take up your cross and walk with Him.

Self, Jesus gave you His life, His all,
Think about that, and kneel in awe.

<u>Acts 16:31</u> NKJV
So they said, "Believe on the Lord Jesus Christ,
and you will be saved, you and your household."

Slaughter

They slaughtered my King
How could I ever forgive?

They sliced His flesh with whips
Bashed His face with stones
Taunting Him, laughing
His Spirit crushed into pieces
My Lord, Best Friend
How could I ever forgive?

"Save yourself!" They mock
"If you are God like you claim!"
Looking down, weeping
He falls at their feet
Christ, my God,
How could I ever forgive?

Looking at *me*, He cries
"It is you, my love,
Who has traded me in."

"I see you laughing and pointing
As you throw the first stone.
You smear blood on my face
And you spit in my eye.
You say I am your King,
How could I ever forgive?"

"Before I die,
Let me say one last thing
I have done this for you,
In my death comes your life
I have taken your place
Just call on my Name.

I love you
No matter how you have hurt me
Or what you have done.

You say "Save yourself,
If you are God like you claim!"
But my child
In this I am saving you
And I am God like I claim.
I'll be your Risen Savior—

And yes, my dear child,
Of course I forgive."

John 11:25 NKJV
Jesus said to her,
"I am the resurrection and the life.
He who believes in Me,
though he may die, he shall live.

My Refuge, My Rock

I pray for grace and love for our enemies who attack.
Just like You did dear Jesus, with lashes on Your
back.

Yes, You died to give life to hypocrites and traitors—
Dear God, how can You possibly love us haters?

Jesus, I was Your enemy.
But You were broken to be my Refuge, my Rock.

Yes, only made possible by Your Blood—
You welcome me to Your Heavenly Flock.

1 John 4:8 ESV
Anyone who does not love does not know God,
because God is love.

An Heir

Sin saturated my spirit,
Flooding my whole being.
Couldn't rid this horror from my mind,
But Someone came to me—

**You saw me at my weakest,
Eaten up by despair,
But Your Blood, Jesus, Your Blood—
Has made me an heir!**

Son of God, Jesus Christ!
You *became* our ultimate sacrifice!
Faith in Your Blood, Lordship, and resurrection—
Welcomes us inside the narrow gate of Heaven!

Ephesians 2:13 ESV
But now in Christ Jesus you who once were far off
have been brought near by the blood of Christ.

Terrifying Cross

Jesus, You didn't come to judge
But rather to serve and pour out Your Blood.

You paid the debt of the world's immorality,
    Offering life and hope to all humanity.

    Yes Jesus, because You care so deeply for the
    lost,
You were tortured and killed on that terrifying
Cross—

    Exactly as predicted in the Scriptures, You are
    now risen!
Upon our belief, You free Your people from Satan's
prison!

    You call us to be a people of faith, a people of
    love—
A people who follow You—who You've washed in Your Blood.

1 John 4:10 KJV
Herein is love, not that we loved God, but that he loved us,
and sent his Son to be the propitiation for our sins.

Dear Self,
You Only Have One Master

Dear Self, the very same hands that formed man at creation,

Are the very same hands that bought your salvation—

His Blood gushed out—Wait, what is this all about?
Your forever life, dear Self, just put your faith in Christ—

Talkin' bout how Jesus is Lord, and He came to rescue this world.
And that He died and rose in your place, just ask'n for faith—

He is the Son of God, your risen Savior—don't put this decision off 'til later.
Dear Self, who do you believe in? Who do you trust will bring you freedom?

Self, the choice is yours, just please don't delay or ignore.
You only serve one master, is it the world? Or Jesus, the Lord?

1 John 3:9 NIV
No one who is born of God will continue to sin,
because God's seed remains in them; they cannot go on sinning,
because they have been born of God.

The Element of Belief:

His Unleashed Power

Chapter 5
The Element of Belief: His Unleashed Power

"Stuff 'n' Things..."

Psalm 27:1 NLT

The Lord is my **LIGHT** and my SALVATION—
so *why* should I be afraid?
The Lord is my **fortress**, <u>protecting</u> me from danger,
so why should I tremble?

Check This Out!

I wish this verse came to mind when I was on the island of Dominica! The group my husband and I traveled with found ourselves in the rainforest on a long, rickety swinging bridge over a football field high. Couldn't see the ground below the treetops. Remember, I can't even stand on a wimpy 2-step ladder with a handle without breaking a sweat. I'm helpless if Danny hides the mixed nuts on the top shelf of the kitchen cabinet. Yes, if you know me, that's serious business.

Finding it comical that I was so terrified on the bridge, Danny stayed behind me, *jumping*. So what happens? The group crosses. I completely *freeze*. Then I feel footsteps *thumping* on the bridge, rushing towards me from behind. Danny is running up to me. He grips my arms. Pushing me. Forcing me to run despite my terror. Ideas devour my mind. Will we rock this thing until it falls apart? Will I fall from this pathetic excuse of a bridge? Will they find me at the bottom? Or will my body be gone forever?

You'll never believe what happened. You got it! I made it to the other side. Yeah, kinda melodramatic, huh? What? I never promised an exhilarating grand finale!

My Guts:

On that bridge, my eyes weren't on the Cross. They were on the rickety bridge and the dark abyss I believed I would fall into. I'm sure I was praying endlessly, but true faith was nowhere to be found. This reminds me of an analogy someone once pointed out. Faith in Jesus as our Savior isn't a simple belief He exists. Faith is trusting Him with your very life as if you are walking off a cliff and Jesus is the bridge Himself. Boy, do I wish I was focusing on Jesus that day!

Question Is...

Jesus's Blood purchased your soul on the Cross!
Question is, "How do you respond?"

Do you believe in Jesus's death and resurrection?
The Son of God, His role in salvation?
It's all about faith, my friend, not perfection.

Faith gives you forever life?
Will you ultimately let Him take the wheel in
your life?

**Yes, Jesus's Blood purchased your soul on the Cross!
Question is, "How do you respond?"**

Genesis 15:6 NIV
**Abram believed the LORD, and he credited it to him as
righteousness.**

Beckon

Your Blood beckons my belief,
From beyond the grave, Your Crimson Flood
screams—
You are most certainly alive,
And it is my very soul You have saved!

I have seen You in action,
Miracles a dead guy can't do,
I have seen You in Your glory,
Yes, I trust in Your redemption story!

You say belief in You, Lord Jesus,
As the very Son of God,
Is all I need for salvation,
No, my works just won't do,
Let me shout this good news to the nations!
Not just a select few!

Hebrews 11:6 ESV
And without faith it is impossible to please him,
for whoever would draw near to God must believe
that he exists and that he rewards those who seek him.

The Kiln

Your kiln-fire consumes me
    Perfecting me—Completing me—
        Painfully growing me into
            The disciple You want me to be—

            My life as clay—You shape and mold
        Then the scorching fire in Your kiln polishes
        me as gold
    At times, refinement comes through grief and woe
But again and again, Jesus proves He will protect me so.

Yes, Your kiln-fire is preparing me for more—
    I have faith You have something truly awesome in store!
        Still feel ill-equipped to stomach such storms—
            But You are my strength, full of missions I
            cannot ignore!

        So, yes, Jesus—I choose to follow You alone, my
        Lord!

Isaiah 6:8 ESV
And I heard the voice of the Lord saying,
    "Whom shall I send, and who will go for us?"
Then I said, "Here am I! Send me."

The Proof that I am His

Jesus, my precious Lord Jesus!
Yes! Total perfection You are!
You are God's Only Son incarnate,
Holding the only key to my pardon,
Offering grace to all who believe—

No, I'm nowhere near perfect,
But my Risen Savior is!
He adopted me into His Kingdom—
—Faith in Jesus, the Son of God,
Proves I am His!

<u>Acts 4:12</u> ESV
And there is salvation in no one else,
for there is no other name under heaven
given among men
by which we must be saved.

Wait Upon Me

I grieve—I have nothing admirable
To offer You, Lord.
My spirit suffers in tangled knots
Demanding answers from within—

How can I possibly bring You glory?
No answer seems to suffice.
I am distraught by my limitations,
Collecting only broken dreams
As I fail You time and again.

Jesus, Your voice speaks lovingly to my soul saying:
"My beloved, I have made My decision!
I set you apart for true Godly missions.
Turn from your countless dreams, and
Wait upon Me."

Jesus! So patient, so kind!
I long to live in Your Holy design!
And I have faith in what hasn't
Yet been revealed at this time—

So wherever You may lead me,
Whatever blessings or horrors I face,
Help me to forever exalt You,
Lord!
Until Your praises are all I can taste!

Jeremiah 29:11 NIV
"For I know the plans I have for you,"
declares the LORD, "plans to prosper you and not to harm you,
plans to give you hope and a future."

Raw Repentance:

Answering the Door

Chapter 6
<u>Raw Repentance</u>: Answering the Door

"Stuff 'n' Things…"

Psalm 5:12 NIV
Surely, Lord,
> You bless the righteous;

You surround them with your favor as with a shield.

Check This Out!

Would I do it again? You bet! I was told my car spiraled in the air a few times before flipping repeatedly on the ground. I found myself in a Medivac helicopter. Ooooh fun! Too bad I couldn't look out the window…Yeah, I was in shock.

No, not my fault. A minivan making a left turn had plowed into my driver's side door. The next thing I heard was, "Is she dead?" You know how they say unconscious people can hear you? I learned first-hand it's true. At one point, I woke up with pieces of my windshield in my eyes. But then I was out again.

My husband Danny recognized a name on the witness list. She was following right behind my car when the other driver crashed into me. So what's the big deal, anyway? Fast forward to two years later. Danny and I were at the bowling alley and we saw the witness. She had a 2-year-old son. This woman was pregnant during the accident. I'm 99% sure if I wasn't there, she would've been in my place and had gotten hit. Would she have lost the baby? God only knows. But I firmly believe God used me to spare the life of that child. So of course, despite the horror, I'd do it again in a heartbeat. In my ignorance, I wasted two years being angry at that driver who hit me. Now I praise God for it. Surely God's presence was with me and that child that day.

Q: In what ways do you see God working in your life? I can assure you if you have given your life to Him, He is active in your life whether you see it or not...

Dare Ya!

Are you bitter about a situation like I was? If so, when you're ready, give your sin to God like I had to. You may learn the truths behind it tomorrow, in two years, when you're old and brittle, or never. However hard, I encourage you to let go and give it to God. I just prayed for you. You're not alone.

Hostage

I want You to be my highest priority, God,
But right now it feels like I'm just a two-faced fraud.
I could ask You to re-ignite my soul - already rotting
with flies,
As I pretend I've stopped believing the Father of Lies.

I long to know You as my loving Protector
Because I've grown into nothing but a foolish idolator.
The passion I once shared with You, my dear precious Lord,
Is sadly disintegrating inside its own private world.

Not fully sure if I care to break free from
these chains,
But my heart surely aches as I play this
senseless game.
Jesus, I do thirst to be Yours again,
Yet I still cling tightly to this
tantalizing sin.

Will I forever be held hostage by this seductive lure?
Oh dear God, restore our relationship to how we once were!
Yes, dear Savior, I beg You, please—
Draw me quickly to the ground on humbled knees!

Revelation 2:5 NIV
Consider how far you have fallen! Repent and do
the things you did at first. If you do not repent,
I will come to you and remove your lampstand from its place.

Imprisoned

Jesus, I've failed You once again.
Ensnared. Imprisoned. Worse than it's ever been.
You were once my Best Friend,
Dear God! When will I choose You over this sin?!

You say the battle is won,
Then why is my soul still rotting and numb?

I have purposely chosen this
broken road,
Turning against You as my life slowly
implodes.
No, don't want to continue to treasure
this world.
Yes, I'm still mourning over Your presence,
Jesus, my Lord.

Acts 3:19 NLT
Now repent of your sins and turn to God,
so that your sins may be wiped away.

Relinquish

I knew my sin would soon
Hang me out to dry.
Too hard to walk away,
So I figured, why try?

But now I'm sick of this game.
Christ has given me a new name.
Time to live up to my God-given potential.
Yes, my walk with Christ is surely essential.

My Jesus, I miss You.
I want to get serious again.
So right now, to the best of my ability,
To You, I relinquish my sin.

Luke 15:7 NLT
In the same way, there is more joy in heaven over one lost sinner who repents and returns to God than over ninety-nine others who are righteous and haven't strayed away!

Burning Coals

Lord, I want to love You
With all of my heart, soul, and mind!
But I'm afraid my faith is starting to stagger behind;
Is my light burning out?
I must say I don't fully doubt.

I'm too ashamed for You to see who I have become,
My heart, soul, and spirit have grown terribly numb—
But no, Jesus, Your specialty is forgiveness and mercy
So I crawl to You with utmost humility.

Lord, search my entire being!
And set ablaze all that offends You, my King!
I have learned first-hand that Satan is
a liar!
So for me, dear Jesus—
Chuck extra coals on him in the fire!!!

Jeremiah 24:7 NLT
I will give them hearts that recognize me as the LORD.
They will be my people, and I will be their God,
for they will return to me wholeheartedly.

Crushed

The wise men brought You
        Gold, frankincense, and myrrh.
When sadly all I can offer is sin,
        And this all-consuming carnal lure.

        My God, I crawl to You now,
As humble as the tax collector.
    Trapped in my sin,
Fully ensnared and tethered—

So to the best of my ability,
      I beg You, Lord, take me now,
Yes, You were crushed for my sin—
        And will someday grant me a crown.

Isaiah 53:5 NLT
But he was pierced for our rebellion,
      crushed for our sins.
He was beaten so we could be whole.
        He was whipped so we could be healed.

Travesty

My heavy heart bleeds full honesty;
Revealing my captive-held soul,
As it grew into nothing but travesty
In this prison...no chance of parole.

Corruption. Lies.
Now admitted freshly to Your Throne.
Only Your mercy can save me now,
A heart slowly beating into stone.

Spirit evolving to lukewarm, my towering sin.
Am I nothing but a foolish God-hater?
The holy separated from the wicked;
Divided so precisely as with a razor.

I say I want You to be my Lord;
No willingness of personal sacrifice in sight.
I cling desperately to this awful world.
Oh God! Please! Drag me into Your light!

As I plead for righteousness,
My spirit aches to know You once again;
To be my One and Only,
My spiritual Best Friend.

The terror lifts in the wake of this tragedy,
As You reignite my soul in the midst of my travesty.
But now I can breathe once again,
As I live in Him.

2 Corinthians 7:10 ESV
**"For Godly grief produces a repentance that leads to salvation
without regret, whereas worldly grief produces death."**

All Along

At times when I turn from You,
I don't even recognize myself as lost.
I forget Your passionate love
That You poured out on the cross.

But when You humble me to
Repentance and call me Your very own,
I bow in awe of Your mercy
As You re-ignite my soul!

Trying to hold it together—
Did I almost lose my Best Friend?
Face down in the glory of Your splendor,
I cry, "Jesus, I am Yours again!"

But Lord, You retort, "*No. Not again*—
Although you were in the wrong,
I would never, ever leave you—
I was right here with you—yes, all along."

Ephesians 1:7 NIV
In him we have redemption through his blood,
the forgiveness of our trespasses,
according to the riches of his grace,

Embracing Grace:

The Open Door

Chapter 7
Embracing Grace: The Open Door

"Stuff 'n' Things..."

Psalm 62:1-2 NIV

Truly my soul finds rest in GOD;
My salvation comes from Him.
Truly He is my **rock and my salvation**;
He is my fortress, I will <u>never</u> be
shaken.

<u>Big Daddy</u>! You knew I would be Yours before I existed. God, people are walking around today who are lost. But I praise You because some of those people are destined to be Your children someday. So, whatever I do, Big Daddy, let it be in love. The most screwed-up person may soon be my brother or sister in Christ.

I know 100% I didn't seem "savable" before You called me. But You worked through loving, obedient people. And I owe You my everything! My entire life! My all! I love You for Your mercy. I praise You! And thank You! Because without You, I'd be forever lost—In Jesus's Name—"

Living a Lie

I still carry the shame You've delivered me from—
    Sometimes it feels like Satan has
    already won.
    Failing to earn my own salvation - so
    terrified to die!
        But Jesus, You speak tenderly to my heart:

I've been believing a lie.

    Feels like my lungs will soon breathe Satan's
    fire.
But no! Jesus has exposed Satan as a deceitful liar!

        Lord, You teach me Your ways,
            And that Your Cross alone
            saves,
        Exposing one of Satan's most
        famous lies:
        Yes, denying the mercy of Jesus
        Christ!
But my Jesus says the battle has already
been won.

**So with Satan, I'm done.
I choose to trust in the Blood of
Jesus, God's Son.**

Lamentations 3:22-23 NIV
Because of the LORD's great love
we are not consumed,
for his compassions never fail.
They are new every morning;
great is your faithfulness.

Giving In?

This spiritual quest
I may never win
Plagued by doubt
Prepared to give in

—Wait, I tend to forget
Your grace is sufficient!
And earning my salvation,
Just simply isn't.

I refuse to waste Your offer of mercy
Because YOU PAID THE DEBT for my eternity!
So I spill my guts at my precious Savior's feet
Confessing my sin, as You welcome me in.

1 John 4:15 NLT
All who declare that Jesus is the Son of God
have God living in them, and they live in God.

On Humbled Knees

Holy Spirit, breathe Your fire deep into my soul!
As surely as You live, most High God,
I will soon rejoice around Your Throne!

Let me forever focus beyond this perishable life!
And always fixate my eyes on You alone,
My dear, precious Jesus Christ!

You, Lord, will never *ever* leave me,
So I pray I honestly mean this with every fiber of my
being,
No matter the cost, or whatever it means—

Help me to fully offer You my soul, Lord. I'm on
humbled knees.

Hebrews 10:23 NIV
Let us hold unswervingly to the hope we profess,
for he who promised is faithful.

Anointed

On this very day, You have given me spiritual power!
Anointed with oil, no longer a coward.
You breathe Your Light into the depths of my soul,
Precious God, like a roaring river—
Yes, let Your Light flow—

You say others will flock to me,
But Hallelujah, it is only *Your* glory they see!
Oh, I used to be rotten to the core,
But You call me to be much, much more!

I was the lost, but You have lavished me with mercy!
You have bestowed blessing upon blessing!
Grace only comes through Your Blood, my Lord,
My God, I depend solely on You in this spiritual war!

I just cannot ignore Your calling!
Overlooking the lost would be simply appalling!
My Savior, I call on the Blood You outpoured!
As You harvest lost souls through me, Jesus, my Lord.

Matthew 9:37 ESV
Then he said to his disciples,
"The harvest is plentiful, but the laborers are few;

Not as it Seems

I thought wholeheartedly that I was His,
But not everything is as it seems it is.
Starting to question my own salvation
Have I retreated into a spiritual vacation?
Now terrified about my ultimate fate
What did I do wrong? Am I too late?

Precious Jesus Christ,
How could I forget Your Sacrifice?
Your death, blood, burial, resurrection?
Son of God, You will *always* be my
salvation!
Am I still missing what You're all
about?
No! Your scars leave no room for
doubt!

Romans 5:8 NIV
But God demonstrates his own love for us in this:
While we were still sinners, Christ died for us.

Worn Around the Edges

Yes, I am worn around the edges,
Frayed *through* and *through—*

Jesus didn't fix my baggage,

He's designing me
COMPLETELY new!

Oooh! I can't wait
to see what my Savior is up to!

Matthew 5:14-16 NKJV
You are the light of the world. A city that is set on a hill cannot
be hidden. Nor do they light a lamp and put it under a basket, but
on a lampstand, and it gives light to all *who are* in the house. Let
your light so shine before men, that they may see your good works
and glorify your Father in heaven.

Under No Other Authority

Jesus,

Because of Your compassion,
With You, my sins were buried,
Under no other Authority—
Is my lawyer, judge, and jury.

Yes! You have set me free!
By the Blood of the Lamb!
Under no other Authority,
Just You, Son of Man!

Hallelujah! Hallelujah!
You have risen from the grave!
Conquering death and Satan,
No more reason to be afraid!

Faith in You Jesus,
You promised my soul to save,
Under no other Authority—
Yes, You alone I praise!

Psalm 103:12 NKJV
As far as the east is from the west,
***So* far has He removed our transgressions from us.**

Deadly Reality

Jesus, remind me of the story
    Of the day You redeemed me
On that ol' Bloody tree!

Because I'm sadly forgetting—
    Yes, forgetting,
What it all means.

        Starting to doubt the power of Your
        Blood,
    And question Your ever-forgiving love!
        I crawl to You in this deadly reality
        of doubt—
    Dear God! Rush to me! What is this all
    about?!

Your Word speaks of Your mercy and grace,
    But I'm too ashamed to even lift up my face.
So You remind me of the deadly reality of Your Cross,
    And my sins You paid for, at the most
    terrifying cost.

Hebrews 9:14 NKJV
How much more shall the blood of Christ,
who through the eternal Spirit offered Himself without spot to God,
cleanse your conscience from dead works to serve the living God?

Divine Pardon

My innocent Substitute bought my life on a tree;
Shortly before His arrest, He prayed for me.
I am mystified by His selfless love,
Here to serve and pour out His Blood.

I was struggling alone in utter shame—
But no! Your nails defeated my blame!
Only You were qualified to pay that steep price—
You alone Jesus *became* my ultimate Sacrifice!

My Jesus! Faith in Your sacrifice alone, will I
glory!
Such a Divine pardon to those who know my story;
Your mercy stirs my soul to shine like the sun!
I praise You Jesus! For the battle is already won!

Your loving presence makes all else disappear—
So beautiful You are, just brings me to tears.
Jesus, Son of God, You have saved my life!
So I will forever praise You, my cherished Jesus Christ!

Revelation 3:20 NIV
Here I am! I stand at the door and knock.
If anyone hears my voice and opens the door,
I will come in and eat with that person, and they with me.

Just Be

I find myself chasing mission after mission
Ignoring Your voice when I'm just called to
listen,
So right now, Jesus I am waiting on Your Word
To clear a path for my upcoming
works—

But no, Your loving voice speaks the truth!
You call me to stop and just *be* with You
Remaining in Your presence with an undivided
heart
Only then will You mold me into Your true piece of art.

You are the only One I choose to pursue
Offering You my whole heart and
starting anew.

Psalm 73:28 NIV
But as for me, it is good to be near God.
I have made the Sovereign Lord my refuge;
I will tell of all your deeds.

Genuine Praise:

Admiring His Ways

Chapter 8
Genuine Praise: Admiring His Ways

"Stuff 'n' Things…"

<u>Psalm 121:1-2</u> ESV

I lift up my eyes to the hills.

From where does my help come?

My help comes from the LORD,

Who *made* <u>heaven</u> and <u>earth</u>.

<u>Big Daddy</u>!

My God! My love! My help! My shelter! May You, God, be absolutely glorified through every part of my life! May I worship You the way You desire! Lord, You lift up my face— By Your own Son's Blood, You call me righteous. Your love is such a beautiful mystery! When You call me Home, I will be speechless. Drowning in tears of joy. Yes, I will fall on my face in the presence of Your splendor. I fearfully and humbly long to see Your brilliance in all its fullness! May I sit in front of Your Throne and just gaze upon You, my Master, and take in Your beauty—forever and ever—"

<u>My Guts</u>

Since I became a believer, I've always prayed to Jesus. Just noticed after all these years, people pray to The Heavenly Father. I realize I'm uncomfortable with "Father." You may have noticed I use the term Big Daddy. I prayerfully chose that term so I wouldn't find Him so scary. It worked. The point? God is not rigid. He created us to be different. I can call Him Big Daddy and dance His praises to Christian rock. And the next guy can hum His praises while tapping on a xylophone with chopsticks. We're all different. And that's okay. God made us that way. So belt out your voice or share your passion with the Lord in thought, but remember, God is good. He deserves to be praised!

Dare Ya!

This might be fun. Choose to praise God differently today. Time is not a factor. Whatever suits you. Try something new. Song? Dance? Poetry? Letter? Prayerfully ask God what He would appreciate. Make sure it's meaningful.

I Bow Down to Your Name

You have given me everything I could ever ask for—
Coincidence? Not a chance!
No one else is fit to wear Your nail-scarred hands!
Yes, in my life I have experienced many crises,
But You, precious Jesus, have blessed me with true inner peace.

My life is worth living solely because of You, my Lord!
Without You, I'd be an oyster...yes, dead with no pearl.
But You, Jesus, have called me to be the salt of the earth—
You have given me a second chance! A spiritual rebirth!

I am drawn to You, Lord Jesus, yes, as a lowly sinner.
But those times I fail You, in Your eyes, I'm still a winner.
Your mercies shower over me day after day,
And for that, my Lord, I bow down to Your Name!

A beautiful Savior! Your brilliance blows me away!
Can't wait to see Your full splendor in Heaven someday!
You, dear precious Jesus, are my King and my Rock.
Oh! I am so grateful You opened my heart when You knocked!

Colossians 3:17 ESV
And whatever you do, in word or deed, do everything in the name
of the Lord Jesus, giving thanks to God the Father through him.

Worthy is the Lamb!

Rejoice, sweet Jesus! Jump to Your feet!
Dance to my praises as all of heaven sings!
Worthy is the Lamb of all honor and esteem!
So I choose to serve the One true God,
Jesus my King!

Loving Jesus, cling to my spirit, heart,
mind, and soul.
Claim them as Your very own—Yes, Yours alone.

Psalm 149:3 ESV
Let them praise his name with dancing,
making melody to him with tambourine and lyre!

Publicity Stunt

You know this ain't no publicity stunt,
Yes, my Father, may my heart just be blunt?
I want to praise You in the way You desire.
You know, like I once did, when I was Your holy livewire—

The stench of my sin left my soul dead and rotting.
But the beauty of Your love defies all boundaries!
Your Son's very own Blood has set me free!
So my face falls flat on the ground as I drop to my knees—

Oh! So eager to walk with You hand-in-hand in Heaven,
Solely because Your Son's Blood has purchased my freedom!
This love You hold for me, I just cannot fathom!
Because for me, Your Son died, and Your heart was shattered.

So, my God, if I may ask one thing,
May You fill my soul with Your praises
As I forever dance around Your feet.

Hebrews 12:28 ESV
Therefore let us be grateful for receiving a kingdom that
cannot be shaken, and thus let us offer to God acceptable
worship, with reverence and awe,

Incense

As the aroma of my praises
Burn as incense at Your Throne,
My Lord, dance to these melodies
Meant for You alone!

My Majestic God, You single-handedly
Assigned the placement of the stars,
Yet for some wild reason,
You still seek out my wayward heart.

Psalm 100:2 ESV
Serve the LORD with gladness!
Come into his presence with singing!

Could Not Ask for More!

God, You used to find me in my private quarters
        Belting out Your praises until overcome by tears!
        But sadly, again, my knees must humbly
        hit the floor—
Spirit, re-ignite my soul more potent than *ever* before!

As I cling to the Cross ever so
intimately
Let it be You alone that others see in me!
My Father! My Savior! My
purpose! My Flame!
May I forever rejoice and glorify Your
Name!

Abba Father, even as such a tremendous Entity,
        You still called Your own Son to die—*instead of me!*
        So as You ask me to forfeit the luxuries of this
        world,
I think of the Cross and no, God—
        I could not ask for more!

Psalm 63:3-4 NIV
Because your love is better than life,
my lips will glorify you.
I will praise you as long as I live,
        and in your name I will lift up my hands.

You Alone

Father, You alone forfeited Your Son's life *for me* by choice,
So to You, Father God, I will forever lift up my voice!
Father, You alone put *my* needs above Your Son,
He conquered death for every nation, tribe, and tongue!

Spirit, You alone breathed fire into my being,
Precious Lord, my God, I fall to my knees!
Spirit, You alone convicted my soul,
And at that salvation moment, my very heart You stole!

Jesus, You alone bled and died on *my* cross,
So in Your honor, I'll surely fight for the Lost!
Jesus, You alone saved mankind with Your hands,
No more need to sacrifice the blood of a ram—

Precious Trinity, You alone are Three-in-One,
Yes, Father, Spirit, Son—
Precious Trinity, You alone are omnipotent,
All for one. One for all. Yet fully independent.

John 10:30 ESV
I and the Father are one.

Upside Down

A cherished Savior
A devoted Son
A loving Bridegroom
A spiritual Best Friend

You are a Treasure to so many people!
So precious—so loved—so sweet—
Your radiant love shines from within You,
Then it floods from Your whole being!

You model the love of our Father,
And have never let us down—
You obey His call to harvest His
Army,
And have turned my world upside down!

With loving inspiration,
Your cross excites me to Your salvation!
Jesus, You fulfill the Bible's redemption
decree—
Devoted Savior!! Your Blood aches for ALL to
believe!

Psalm 106:1 NIV
Praise the LORD.
Give thanks to the LORD, for he is good;
his love endures forever.

Rags to Royalty

Precious Jesus, You are the Author of my salvation,
The Redeemer of my soul.
Let me shout it out to the nations!

You are omnipotent and have no equal,
Yet You pour out Your heart to a
hateful people.

Beloved Jesus, You pursued me when I was
dead in sin.
Now You are my Faith, my Hope, my Salvation, my
Friend!

Precious Jesus, my Lord! I owe You for all
that I am—
Purchased from rags to Royalty, by the Blood of the
Lamb.

Psalm 146:1-2 NKJV
Praise the Lord! Praise the Lord, O my soul!
While I live I will praise the Lord;
I will sing praises to my God while I have my being.

Consumed

My Lord Jesus, Your beauty
Cannot be bound by words.
My spirit sings of Your love
In a language I've never learned—

I beg for Your presence
To consume my entire being.
A Spirit so precious,
Be fully mine, flawless Deity.

Father, You placed a price tag on our souls
The Blood of Your very own Son
Your pain was more real than I can fathom
Yes, Father, You allowed Him to bleed out—
So You can call repentant sinners Your *children*.

Psalm 30:11 NLT
You have turned my mourning into joyful dancing.
You have taken away my clothes of mourning
and clothed me with joy,

An Unraveling Mystery!

Your Scripture excites me like an unraveling mystery!
So enchanting, so captivating—How can it not be?

I grow increasingly engulfed flipping page to page!
Clinging to Your Word to ensure I win this race.

I revere Your Scripture and hold it in high esteem!
Because You opened my eyes that I may believe.

<u>Hebrews 4:12</u> NLT
For the word of God is alive and powerful.
It is sharper than the sharpest two-edged sword,
cutting between soul and spirit, between joint and marrow.
It exposes our innermost thoughts and desires.

Totally Won Me Over!

Through faith, You credit me as blameless!
By Your Sacrifice alone, I will not die nameless—
My name is in Your Lamb's Book of Life!
All because Your cross destroyed evil's fight!

You died to save a hateful, sinful world—
And for that, You totally won me over, Lord!
No doubt You have risen!
Yes, You freed my chains from Satan's prison!

Your offer of grace is wholly unfathomable!
For one to ignore it, would be a dangerous gamble!

Jesus, You are the Author of life and salvation!
Your Cross has triumphed over death and Satan!
I am solely alive in You! The proof is in Your Scars!
Your praises consume me! Oh, how I love who You are!

Romans 8:1-2 NIV
Therefore, there is now no condemnation for those who are in Christ Jesus, because through Christ Jesus the law of the Spirit who gives life has set you free from the law of sin and death.

Live Wire

When You first invited me in,
I was instantly hooked!
Overcome by Your splendor,
And absorbed in Your Book!

Holy Spirit, You have
Filled me with Godly fire!
So I ask of You again, transform me
Back into that Holy livewire!

Psalm 95:6 NIV
Come, let us bow down in worship,
let us kneel before the LORD our Maker;

Spectacular!

Your Spirit ignites my soul brighter than lightning!
Laughing because Satan finds You dreadfully
frightening!
Your Holy Word booms more powerful than thunder!
As those of us You save, bow in wonder!

Hear my praises surround Your Heavenly Throne!
And dance to these melodies meant for You alone!---
As long as I live, I will lift up my voice!
Bursting with praises! Yes! In You, I rejoice!

My Lord, You fill me with excitement and awe!
Never a dull moment when I give You my all!
I've experienced You first-hand, and can testify for sure—
There's no competition! You are undeniably spectacular!

Hebrews 13:15 NKJV
Therefore by Him let us continually
offer the sacrifice of praise to God,
that is, the fruit of *our* lips, giving thanks to His name.

Tender Authority

You formed dirt into man
And bought the world's salvation
With Your hands,
You breathed life into my being
So to You Jesus, all praises I bring!

Precious Jesus, I adore who You are—
But I will never understand the love in Your
heart!
You are the sole Authority
Over all the universe and beyond!
Yet still as tender as a mother deer with
her fawn.

My hope rests in You, loving Majesty! Amen!
Your Blood is more potent than all of my sin!
Can't grasp the mystery of Your saving grace!
So I sing of Your glory until it's all I can taste!

Isaiah 25:1 NKJV
O LORD, You *are* my God.
I will exalt You,
I will praise Your name,
For You have done wonderful *things;*
***Your* counsels of old *are* faithfulness *and* truth.**

The One Authentic Savior

My Jesus, my love for You will never fail.
After all, it was You who bore *my* nails!
Your tender heart bewilders my soul.
You obeyed our Father and made me whole.
I praise You, Jesus! For Your love has won!
You gave me a jumpstart when I was rotten and numb.
I adore who You are, I can't say it enough!
You gave Your life willingly,
No need to be cuffed.

You still walk with me day in, and day out,
Even the hairs on my head You count!
I trust You, dear Lord, even when I think I don't.
You've proven Your loyalty, I know You won't bolt.
When all is said and done, I know You are faithful.
Even the times I feel downright hateful.
Although at times our relationship ebbs and flows,
I will continue to cling to You, as You hold me close.

Psalm 98:4-6 ESV
Make a joyful noise to the LORD, all the earth;
break forth into joyous song and sing praises!
Sing praises to the LORD with the lyre,
with the lyre and the sound of melody!
With trumpets and the sound of the horn
make a joyful noise before the King, the LORD!

Your Spotlight

I want to treasure You with boundless devotion,
Lord!
So fill me with contagious love like never before!

Lord, I ask to adjust the *spotlight* - yes, all
eyes on You!
And through You alone, Jesus may I
bear much fruit!

So as I cling to You ever so intimately,
Let it only be You that others see in me!

Flood me to overflowing with
Your Holy Spirit!
As I share to all who will utterly
revere it—

Help me expose the depth of Your loving nature
Revealing Your true Self: There is no one
greater!

Mark 16:15 NLT
And then he told them,
"Go into all the world
and preach the Good News to everyone.

Your Living Word

My spirit lingers on Your every Word!
I become so drawn in—so lured—
You unravel the mysteries of the universe,
Revealing Your true Self, and everything else!

Your Scriptures humble me toward faith and obedience,
No more teetering on Satan's fence!
Hear my praise, Lord Jesus! With You, I am fully smitten!
Because You, my God, inspired the best Book ever written!

Jesus, rejoice in my utmost affection—oh so true!
And embrace my worship that is reserved just for You!
Forever breathe Your living Word into my spirit!
Yes! Beyond my dying day, I will still revere it!

Your Holy Word fulfills Your salvation decree,
So I pray for those who just haven't yet seen—
Jesus, You are the Way, the Truth, and the Life!
The only true Messiah, the One true Christ!

Matthew 7:24 ESV
Everyone then who hears these words of mine and does them
will be like a wise man who built his house on the rock.

Through My Eyes

You LEFT Your **throne** on high
To come as a *Servant* to DIE—
Yet the **risen** Savior You
became!

Jesus, You've given me a *new life*,
a **new name**!
DEFEATING Satan and
revealing his shame!

You are my Healing, my Laughter, my Love!
My perfect, RISEN **God-send** from above!
I wish the **world** could see You THROUGH
my eyes—
To know *why* I choose to **walk** in
Your Light!

And yes, most **loving God,**
You make known—
My soul finds rest in You alone.

<u>Matthew 13:44</u> **NIV**
The kingdom of heaven is like treasure hidden in a field.
When a man found it, he hid it again, and then in his joy
went and sold all he had and bought that field.

Dear Self,
Give Him a Shout Out!

Dear Self, lift up your voice!
Praise Jesus for His Sacrifice, in His Name, rejoice!

Exalt the Lord with all your heart, soul, and mind,
Dear Self, tears are welcome, no need to be shy—

Lift up your hands, Self! Give Him all the glory!
Shout out His praises for your own personal redemption
story!

Self! Before the Lord, I see you fall flat on your face!
Yes! Life is only worth living after experiencing His grace!

<u>Jude 1:25 NIV</u>
**To the only God our Savior be glory, majesty, power and authority,
through Jesus Christ our Lord, before all ages, now and
forevermore! Amen.**

In My Heart

Lord, I want to praise You differently today,
I guess I need to increase my vocabulary.
No, I can think of a better start.
I'll just tell you what's in my heart—

What's in my heart?

I love You more than what's in my online shopping cart.
I love You more than bacon lard.
I love You more than the writing in a greeting card.
I love You more than my brand-new sports car...
Ok, so I don't have a brand-new sports car.
But if I did, I'd love You more!

Psalm 100:1-5 ESV
A Psalm for giving thanks. Make a joyful noise to the LORD, all the earth! Serve the LORD with gladness! Come into his presence with singing! Know that the LORD, he is God! It is he who made us, and we are his; we are his people, and the sheep of his pasture. Enter his gates with thanksgiving, and his courts with praise! Give thanks to him; bless his name! For the LORD is good; his steadfast love endures forever, and his faithfulness to all generations.

Let's Get Real

Jesus, You know who You are to me—

You're not restricted to a poem
Nor dependent on a rhyme,
Not one to be confined
To a slick-sounding line.

No, my Lord Jesus. It's time to get real—

Jesus, I approach You with a sincere, honest, and humble heart—
No, I will never understand the Cross. You know I have nothing to
offer You that is worthy of Your gut-wrenching sacrifice. Yet Your
grace still stands strong. You remind me that where I am limited, Your
glory flourishes. And I celebrate You for that! You are not dependent
on me in any way, but by Your mercy, You call me Your very own.

When You first called me to Your Kingdom, I experienced how easy
it is to fall in love with You. Much more awesome than the world
could ever offer! You see my heart. I want every soul to experience
the beauty of Your salvation! I was nothing without You. Worthless.
But no, You give me a reason to live! A reason to march on!

Jesus, I praise You and love You for who You are! I thank You for
the Cross, because, my precious Jesus, I would be forever broken
without You and forever lost.

Jesus, may You alone receive all the glory throughout my life—
forever and ever. Amen!

Psalm 7:17 NKJV
I will praise the Lord according to His righteousness,
And will sing praise to the name of the Lord Most High.

Dedications:

The Personals

A shout-out to a few special people in my life...

Chapter 9
Dedications: The Personals

"Stuff 'n' Things…"

<u>Psalm 16:8</u> NIV

I keep my eyes <u>always on the Lord</u>.
With Him at my right hand,
I will <u>not</u> be shaken.

Check This Out!
I didn't want to know the answer. I didn't care to know God's opinion. No. I already made my own decision. The plans were made—
Finally, the tension grew within me. My spirit began to buckle. It was time to give the decision to God. I was terrified. "God, is it Your will for me to marry my fiancé, Danny?" Instantly I could see the answer clearer than through polished glass. I was initially surprised at the answer. The deepest sensation of peace fell over my entire body like never before. I did not fully understand how much of a blessing Danny would become back then, but in our 20 years of marriage (and counting), I know now.
It hasn't always been roses and daisies, but God keeps us strong. That man has grown to be the love of my life. However, if God's answer was "no," I can only pray I would've honored His wishes. Because we wouldn't have been blessed—or happy.

My Guts

That story was a personal event from my life about someone special. The next 5 poems are what I call The Personals. Most have been written to particular people in my life. One is written to God on behalf of my parakeet. Yes, he cares about every aspect of our lives! Praise God!

To my sweet husband, Danny. This is the first poem I wrote and it was inspired by my favorite poet, my Grandma Vee.

If You Really Felt My Love

You always say you need to feel loved
You always say you feel my love dearly
But honey
I say if you really felt my love
You would feel my lips kissing your soul
I say if you really felt my love
You would see in my eyes the one red rose
Held just for you

I say if you really felt my love
You would drown in my tears
Spilled from beautiful thoughts of us...

You always say you need to feel loved
You always say you feel my love dearly

But honey
I must say
Although I cherish you from the center of my spirit
Words mean nothing

I must say
Although you are the only one for me
Words mean nothing

So I must pray
I am able to show you my love
That you may always say
You feel my love dearly.

Colossians 3:14 ESV
**And above all these put on love, which binds everything together
in perfect harmony.**

To my dear friend, Sehee. She is the most real, raw, most loving, and Christ-like person I know!

And I Love You for That...

Sehee, when I think of you,
I see a humble woman of faith.
A forever-living sacrifice,
Who reflects God's Spirit
Of love each day...

And I love you for that...

Your walk with Christ is evidence
Of His Holy manifestation,
No games, no nonsense…
Just purebred salvation!

God entrusts you with our many needs…
Knowing they draw you straight to your knees!
And right on time, as if on cue,
Your Christ-like love always shines true...

And I love you for that...

**Thank You, God,
For giving Sehee to the world...
And yes dear Jesus...**

I love You for that!

**John 15:12 ESV
This is my commandment,
that you love one another as I have loved you.**

To my friend, Stacy (name changed). She was adopted as a child and feels abandoned by her adoptive father. Her birth father passed away before she could meet him. Now she relies on her Heavenly Father.

Spiritual Adoption

Father, the quiver in her voice
Speaks volumes to my heart.
Her sorrow is beyond contagious—

—But You, her devoted Father
Favor her as Your treasure,
So You reach for Your daughter's hand
And walk this journey together.

God, only You can measure the
compassion
That is riddled throughout my being!
Convinced of the power of prayer,
I choose to remain before You
on my knees.
Sweet, loving Father, in the midst of her grief,
You are most certainly at work! Yes!
Behind the scenes!

Sometimes You use the storms to reach us,
And suffering is so close to the heart of Your servant, Jesus.
In You, we can lift up our devastated cries,
Because Your Son *became* our sin and laid down His life—
Yes for me, and my precious sister in Christ!

She feels so alone, disconnected from
family,
But Father! You chose to adopt her into Your
Holy Royalty!
No one can convince me of a greater
love—
Her soul's price tag was the Blood
of Your Son!

1 John 3:1 NIV
See what great love the Father has lavished on us,
that we should be called children of God!...

To my big sister, Donna, whom I love from the bottom of my heart. Gotta make this gal happy.

I'd Do Anything

Donna, my sister in Christ, if you'd find it a hoot,
    I'd dance with crocodiles in the Nile!
    Yes, I'd do anything for even a half-cracked smile—
    Sure! You'll have front-row tickets on your home TV,
    And I'll be right there in your living room out of breath on your Wii.

Sis, did I mention if it would light up your face,
I'd mail 30 GIGANTIC sunflowers falling out of an absurdly small vase?
            Yes, I'd do anything to catch just a smirk,
Even paint myself blue and parade around like a Smurf.

Dear Sis, to bring you true happiness, peace, and joy, I will always fall short,
    Even still, I'm willing to look like a major dork.
        But I'd rather us both look up Above,
    But I did say I'd do anything—

So if I'm called to juggle dog eyeballs—
            —Jesus, I need quite a shove.

Romans 13:8 RSV
Owe no one anything, except to love one another;
    for he who loves his neighbor has fulfilled the law.

164

A prayer for my sweet parakeet, Fritter. He was wounded and he lost a lot of blood. This was written before I knew if he would survive. He is healthy and strong, sitting next to me right now...

Fritter

Out of all the requests in this world,
You know my one petition, Lord.
Right now, just keep my Fritter alive,
And override the past terror
That may soon rob him of his life.

No matter his fate, Lord, Your will is mine.
May Fritter's life and death bring You glory divine.
Yes, my Fritter, this blessing You've given,
Now in this emergency, I ask for much wisdom.

I pray his blood loss isn't as dangerous as it seems,
And You, dear God, are at work behind the scenes.
What is Your will, Jesus? I'm quite terrified to know.
Right now my emotions have been trapped in limbo.

1 Corinthians 2:5 ESV
So that your faith might not rest in the wisdom of men but in the power of God.

Grand Finale:

The Take-Away...

Chapter 10
Grand Finale: The Take-Away
Stuff 'n' Things: The Bird
"Stuff 'n' Things..."

Psalm 84:11 RSV

For the **LORD God** is a **sun and shield;**
 He bestows favor and honor;
No good thing does the Lord withhold
 from those who **walk** uprightly.

Check This Out!

My heart sank the morning I practically interrogated my boss
about the situation. A bird at my job at the pet store had been
returned dead. Or, in my opinion, "killed." I was devastated,
worried my favorite pet store bird would be next. To my horror, my
boss admitted the bird I was obsessed with had been sold. She told
me the buyer would pick him up at 6 pm. Then the time came. My
boss brought him to me in his carrier and said he was going to his
new home now. His new owner had come to pick him up. My heart
sank again. I expressed my heartfelt goodbyes to this beloved bird.
So consumed by the moment that I didn't notice all my coworkers
laughing hysterically. I didn't notice the bow on top of the carrier. I
didn't notice the familiar carrier or pattern on the sheet covering it.
And no, I didn't notice my loving husband Danny standing beside
me, smiling from ear to ear. You got it! Actually, no, you didn't. I
got it! Pardon me. I got "him."

My Guts

God never promised a life of worldly luxuries. However, He enjoys
bestowing blessing after blessing, like with this bird; I was smitten.
More importantly, the Lord enjoys lavishing us with spiritual
blessings. Healing, mercy, and salvation are His specialties. We can

remember that Jesus said yes to the cross. For you. For me. Praise God! Our God is a healing God and He calls us to be His children! Imagine that! This last poem sums up this entire book. Read it carefully. Does any of it apply to you? Think about it.

All I'll Ever Be

Hopeless...
All I thought I'd be
Ready to give up,
But Someone came to me...

Broken...
Always thought I'd be
But I hear a soft whisper,
"You're not too far gone for Me..."

Forgiven...
Never thought I'd be
As I pray for dear mercy, I hear,
"My love, you belong to me..."

A child of God...
All I'll ever be
With faith in Your Blood and Lordship, Jesus...
You call me Your masterpiece...

<u>2 Chronicles 30:9</u> **NIV**
...for the LORD your God is
gracious and compassionate.
He will not turn his face from you
if you return to him.

About the Author

Crystal Joy is a believer in Christ who reveals her deepest emotions through her poetry. She brings her struggles with bipolar disorder to life and speaks to groups from behind the microphone with raw honesty.

Printed in the United States
by Baker & Taylor Publisher Services